# PUNCTUATION PARTNERS

## Grades 2 - 4

**Written by Rita Levin**
**Illustrated by Beverly Armstrong**

# The Learning Works

**Edited by Sherri M. Butterfield**

The purchase of this book entitles the individual teacher to reproduce copies for use in the classroom.

The reproduction of any part for an entire school or school system or for commercial use is strictly prohibited.

No form of this work may be reproduced or transmitted or recorded without written permission from the publisher.

# Contents

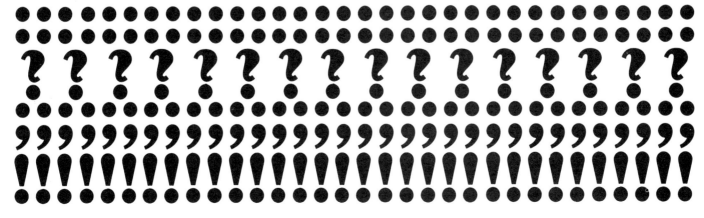

# To the Teacher

In **Punctuation Partners**, seven appealing cartoon characters are used to acquaint students in the second, third, and fourth grades with basic punctuation rules and their applications. On separate pages, Peter Period, Connie Comma, Quentin Question Mark, Eleanor Exclamation Point, Alfred Apostrophe, and the Quotation Mark Twins—Karl and Karla—introduce themselves and explain their use. The book includes

- worksheets on which each punctuation mark is explained and used;
- review sheets to measure student understanding and progress;
- eye-catching mini-posters you can use as reminders of the punctuation partners and the places in which they are needed;
- games and activities for skill reinforcement;
- an answer key for ready reference; and
- an award you can use to recognize students who complete these activities and become "punctuation partners."

**Punctuation Partners** can be used with small groups or with an entire class to teach new skills or to reinforce skills that have been introduced previously.

Name _____

# A Word to the Wise

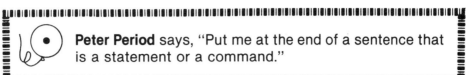

Peter Period says, "Put me at the end of a sentence that is a statement or a command."

Ben Franklin was a famous American. He had many good ideas and invented many useful things. He shared his ideas by giving advice to other people.

Some of the advice Ben Franklin gave is written below. Read the paragraph and put a period at the end of each statement or command. The first one has been done for you.

A word to the wise is enough. Remember that time is money  Little strokes fell great oaks  Lost time is never found again  There are no gains without pains  He that riseth late, must trot all day  A small leak will sink a great ship  The used key is always bright  It is hard for an empty sack to stand upright  Early to bed and early to rise, makes a man healthy, wealthy, and wise

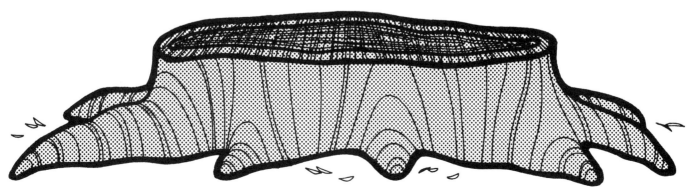

Name _____

# Fractured Fortunes

Something went wrong at the Chinese Dragon Fortune Cookie Company. Everyone who opened a cookie at the Imperial Palace Restaurant one night found the fortune cut in two. The fortunes they found are pictured below.

Find the two parts that go together to form each fortune. Write the complete fortunes on the lines at the bottom of the page. Put **Peter Period** at the end of each statement or command. The first one has been done for you.

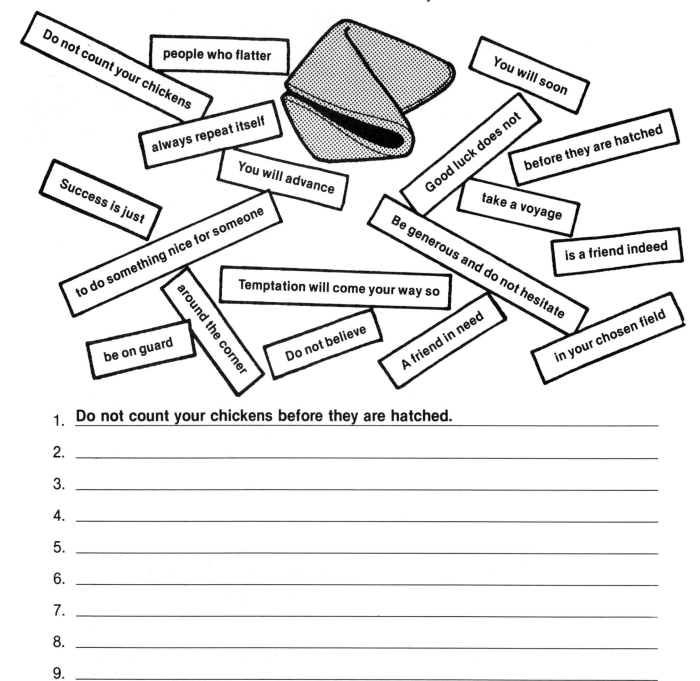

1. **Do not count your chickens before they are hatched.** _____

2. _____

3. _____

4. _____

5. _____

6. _____

7. _____

8. _____

9. _____

Name _____

# The Portrait Gallery

**Peter Period** says, "Put me after an initial or an abbreviation in a person's name."

On the wall below hangs a group of empty picture frames. Read the name at the bottom of each frame. Put **Peter Period** wherever he has been forgotten. He needs to be used at least once in each name. Then draw a picture of each person.

Mr Ted E Bear

Mrs Ima T Vee

Dr E Z Filler

Dr May Pole

Mr Sal T Pretzel

Gov Bob E Pin

Mrs A Turtle

Prof Al E Gator

Sgt Hersh E Bar

Name _____

# Ad Venture

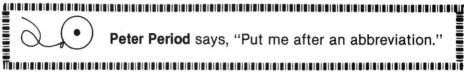

**Peter Period** says, "Put me after an abbreviation."

Each one of these newspaper advertisements contains at least one abbreviation. Read the advertisements, and put **Peter Period** after every abbreviation you find. The number in the upper left-hand corner of the advertisement tells you how many periods are needed.

| | |
|---|---|
| **7**     **GARAGE SALE**<br>Sat , Oct 18, 9 a m – 5 p m<br>100 Sea View Dr | **3**     **FREE TO A GOOD HOME**<br>lovable collie, 2 yrs old, 3712 Chesholm Rd ,<br>all day Sun |

**3**     **FOR SALE**
5400 sq  ft  warehouse
Fast Buck Realty Co

| | |
|---|---|
| **5**     **FOR RENT**<br>2 bedroom apt , 3 blocks N of Hunter Ave<br>Sch                  Ph 964-2852 | **6**     **MR  PINE'S TREE SERVICE**<br>available Mon – Sat<br>reasonable rates<br>Ph  968-6530 after 6 p m |

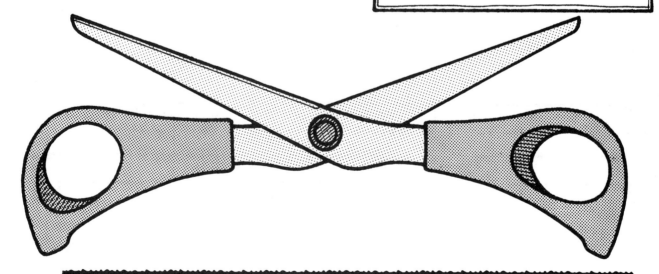

## Try This!
Write your own advertisements. Be sure to include some abbreviations. Ask a friend to put the periods in the proper places.

Name _____

# Crack the Code

**Connie Comma** says, "Put me between the day and year in a date."

Crack the code for each date below. Write the date on the line. Remember to put **Connie Comma** after the day and before the year. The first one has been done for you.

| January | May | August |
|---------|-----|--------|
| July | March | November |
| December | October | April |

| 21 | 4 | 15 |
|----|----|----|
| 3 | 28 | 1 |
| 12 | 16 | 23 |

1982
1880      1990
1972

1. _____ **January 21, 1982** _____

2. _____

3. _____

4. _____

5. _____

6. _____

7. _____

8. _____

9. _____

10. _____

## Try This!

Select four famous people. Write their names on a piece of paper. Look them up in an encyclopedia. Beside the name of each person, write the date he or she was born. Remember to include **Connie Comma** in the proper place.

Name _____

# The Picnic Game

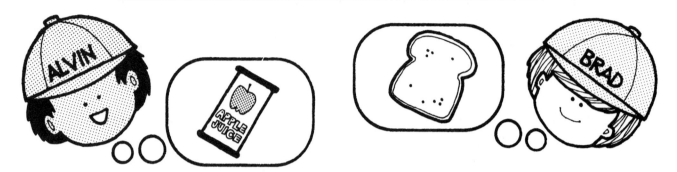

Connie Comma says, "Put me after each item in a series except the last one."

These six children are playing a game called "I'm Going on a Picnic." Each one of them is thinking of the item he or she will bring. The first player starts by saying, "I'm going on a picnic, and I'm bringing . . . . " He or she fills in the name of an item that starts with the letter **a**. The next person repeats what the **a** person said and then adds a **b** item. The third person repeats what the **b** person said and then adds a **c** item. As the game continues, the list gets longer and harder to remember.

Name

# The Picnic Game
## (continued)

Complete each sentence by writing all of the items each person must bring to the picnic. Notice that each person's name and the item he or she is bringing start with the same letter. Be sure to write *and* before the last item, and use **Connie Comma** as often as she is needed. The first sentence has been done for you.

1. Alvin is bringing     **apple juice**                                                    .

2. Brad is bringing                                                                        .

3. Colleen is bringing                                                                     .

4. Donna is bringing                                                                       

                                                                                          .

5. Enid is bringing                                                                        

                                                                                          .

6. Fritz is bringing                                                                       

                                                                                          .

---
**Try This!**
Play "I'm Going on a Picnic" in your class. See if you can get through the entire alphabet. Every time you come to a place where you need **Connie Comma**, draw an imaginary comma in the air with your right hand.
---

Name _____

# Travel Time

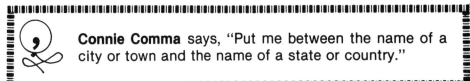

**Connie Comma** says, "Put me between the name of a city or town and the name of a state or country."

Complete each sentence with the correct information. Remember to put **Connie Comma** in the proper place. The first one has been done for you.

1. In 1773, a famous tea party took place in ____**Boston,**_____

   **Massachusetts**_____. (city, state)

2. The Statue of Liberty welcomes visitors in _____

   _____. (city, state)

3. I was born in  _____. (city or town, state or country)

4. The Golden Gate Bridge is one of two large bridges in _____

   _____. (city, state)

5. The Eiffel Tower stands 1,056 feet high in_____

   _____. (city, country)

6. To visit Buckingham Palace and Trafalgar Square, you would have to go to

   _____. (city, country)

7. My mother grew up in  _____. (city or town, state or country)

8. My father grew up in _____. (city or town, state or country)

9. The Astrodome seats 44,500 people in _____. (city, state)

10. I would like to visit _____. (city, state or country)

---

### Try This!
Find some city-state pairs in which both names start with the same letter of the alphabet like *Missoula*, *Montana*, and *Paoli*, *Pennsylvania*. Make a list of these pairs. Be sure that the names are spelled correctly, and remember to put **Connie Comma** between the name of each city and the name of the state in which it is located. See if you can find some of these places on a large map of the United States.

Name _____

# Canvassing the Class

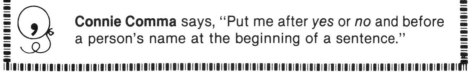

**Connie Comma** says, "Put me after *yes* or *no* and before a person's name at the beginning of a sentence."

Complete the sentences below using the names of some of your classmates. Start each sentence with either *yes* or *no* followed by **Connie Comma** and the person's first name.

1. _____ likes to eat pizza.

2. _____ doesn't ride her bike to school.

3. _____ plays soccer.

4. _____ has a friend in this class.

5. _____ likes to read books about famous people.

6. _____ has at least one brother or sister.

7. _____ didn't go to the movies this month.

8. _____ has attended this school since kindergarten.

9. _____ loves his teddy bear.

10. _____ eats eggs for breakfast.

Name _____

# Meet Connie Comma

**Connie Comma** would like to take this opportunity to tell you a little about herself. Read her short autobiography carefully. She has purposely left out all of the commas. Your job is to use all of the rules she has taught you to discover where the commas belong and to put them in. Connie has one clue for you: there should be twelve commas.

Hi! My name is Constance Comma. My friends call me Connie  Con  or CC. I was born in Juneau  Alaska. I moved to Anchorage when I was three. My birthday is February 29  1980. I celebrate it on March 1  when it's not Leap Year. I'll be twenty years old on February 29  2000. Peter Period  Alfred Apostrophe  Quentin Question mark  Eleanor Exclamation Point  and the Quotation Mark Twins are my best friends. We love to party  play  and punctuate. Yes  I enjoy being a punctuation partner.

## Try This!
Cut a short article from the newspaper. Circle all of the commas. Bring your article to class. Exchange articles with a friend, and check to be sure all of the commas have been circled.

Name _____

# Scrambled Sentences

Put together the words and phrases in the eggs below to make four sentences that tell about poultry. The number in each egg tells you which sentence it belongs to. Copy each complete sentence on the right numbered line at the bottom of the page. Remember to use **Peter Period** and **Connie Comma** when they are needed.

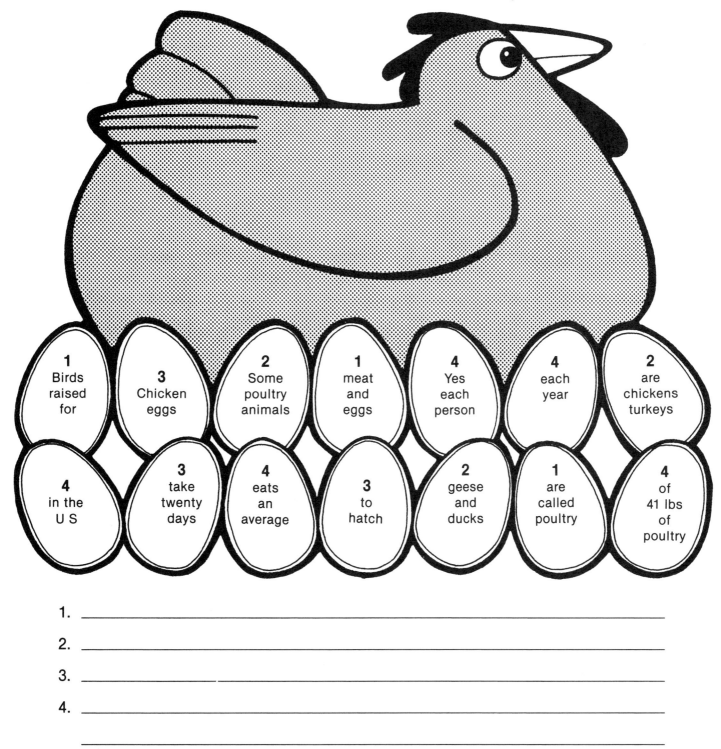

1. _____

2. _____

3. _____

4. _____

_____

Name _____

# Riddle Me

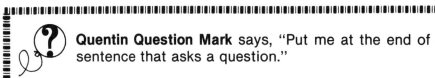

**Quentin Question Mark** says, "Put me at the end of a sentence that asks a question."

These two columns contain a total of ten riddles and the solutions to them. Read each sentence. If it asks a question, put **Quentin Question Mark** at the end. If it gives an answer, put **Peter Period** at the end. Then match each riddle with its solution by drawing a line to connect the two. The first one has been done for you.

How does an elephant get down from a tree **?**

It goes in one ear and out another

I don't give a hoot about you

A stocking does

What did Delaware

It won't be long now

Why did Silly Sally put her father in the refrigerator

Who can raise things without lifting them

A sunburned zebra is

What is the best way to keep fish from smelling

What is black and white and red all over

She wanted a cold pop

What does a worm do in a cornfield

A farmer can

What did the scissors say to the barber

It sits on a leaf and waits until fall **.**

Cut off their noses

What has a heel, a toe, a leg, and nothing else

She wore a New Jersey

What did one owl say to the other owl

## Try This!
Make up or find four riddles. Write them on a piece of paper. Remember to put **Quentin Question Mark** at the end of each one. Bring your riddles to school and exchange riddles with a friend.

Name _____

# Bus Banter

The children in this bus are going on a field trip. They are talking. Read what each one says. If the child is asking a question, put **Quentin Question Mark** at the end. If the child is making a statement, put **Peter Period** at the end.

Name _____

# Stormy Weather

**Eleanor Exclamation Point** says, "Put me at the end of a sentence that shows strong feeling."

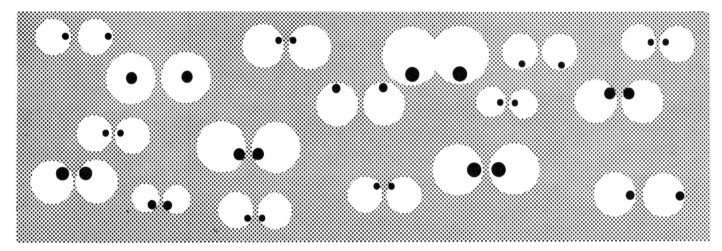

It was two o'clock in the afternoon. Suddenly the sky darkened, and a violent storm broke loose. While Mr. Snow was reading a story to his class, the lights flickered and then went out. These comments were made by some startled members of the class. They show strong feeling, so put **Eleanor Exclamation Point** at the end of each one.

1. How dark the room is

2. Look at that lightning

3. The thunder is rattling the windows

4. Boy, am I scared

5. Listen to the wind howl

6. This is really exciting

Pretend that you are sitting in this classroom. Write four more comments that show strong feeling. Remember to put **Eleanor Exclamation Point** at the end of each one.

7. _____

8. _____

9. _____

10. _____

Name _____

# Cartoon Capers

Look at the four cartoons carefully. Read the four sentences at the bottom of the page. Decide which sentence is being said by which person. Write each sentence in the right bubble. Remember to use **Eleanor Exclamation Point**.

Look at that square dance
Now that's a *real* bookworm

Don't make a spectacle of yourself
Hit the road

Name _____

# A Twist of the Tongue

The final punctuation marks are missing from these tongue twisters. Read each twister carefully. Then put **Peter Period, Quentin Question Mark,** and **Eleanor Exclamation Point** where they are needed.

1. Did Darby dive down deep during December

2. Every eligible elephant eats eggs Easter evening

3. Will Willie and Wilma wind their way west

4. Tina the Terrible took twenty tadpoles today

5. What a wily walrus Waldo was

6. Should Steve sell seventeen small-sized shirts

7. Mischievous Miles makes mud mountains most Mondays

8. Barnaby Badger bowed bashfully before busloads of bankers

9. How happily Harriet Hippo and Herbert Hedgehog harmonized

10. Can cunning Carlos calm cantankerous Carmen

# At the Pet Show

 **Alfred Apostrophe** says, "Put me between a name and an *s* to show ownership."

These children are waiting to show their animals in the Westwood Annual Pet Show. They have spent many days getting ready for this big event. Each one of them is hoping to take home a ribbon. Match each pet with its owner by writing names on the lines on page 22.

Name _____

# At the Pet Show
## (continued)

Read each sentence. Look at the pictures on page 21. Then write the right name on each line. Remember to use **Alfred Apostrophe** and an *s*. The first one has been done for you.

1. ___**Heidi's**___ Angora rabbit eats lots of lettuce.

2. _____ baby lamb is wearing a polka-dot collar.

3. _____ yellow parakeet loves to sing.

4. _____ boa constrictor is ten feet long.

5. _____ beagle sits up and begs.

6. _____ hen lays a big egg every morning.

7. _____ red-eared turtle hibernates each winter.

8. _____ Persian cat is named Blackie.

9. _____ short-haired pointer won first prize at the pet show last year.

10. _____ pet rat likes to perch on his owner's shoulder.

PET WITH THE LONGEST TAIL  MOST ACTIVE PET  NOISIEST PET  MOST UNUSUAL PET  PET WITH THE LONGEST EARS  PET WITH THE MOST SPOTS

Tom's Room

### Try This!
Design a sign for each bedroom in your house or apartment to let people know who sleeps there. Draw pictures on your signs. Remember to use **Alfred Apostrophe** and an *s* on each sign.

Name _____

# Will You Be Mine?

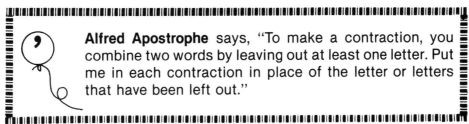

**Alfred Apostrophe** says, "To make a contraction, you combine two words by leaving out at least one letter. Put me in each contraction in place of the letter or letters that have been left out."

Last Valentine's Day, the students in Mrs. Love's class found some funny messages on their heart candies. Somehow the machine that stamps the candies printed only the first letter of the first word of each message. Use the Candy Message Machine below to help you fill in the missing letters. Remember to put **Alfred Apostrophe** where he is needed.

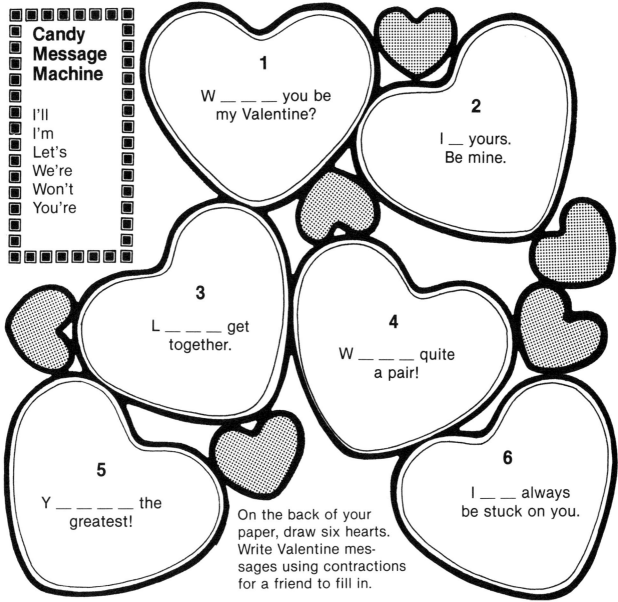

**Candy Message Machine**

I'll
I'm
Let's
We're
Won't
You're

**1**
W _ _ _ _ you be
my Valentine?

**2**
I _ yours.
Be mine.

**3**
L _ _ _ _ get
together.

**4**
W _ _ _ _ quite
a pair!

**5**
Y _ _ _ _ _ the
greatest!

**6**
I _ _ always
be stuck on you.

On the back of your paper, draw six hearts. Write Valentine messages using contractions for a friend to fill in.

Name _____

# The Lunch Bunch

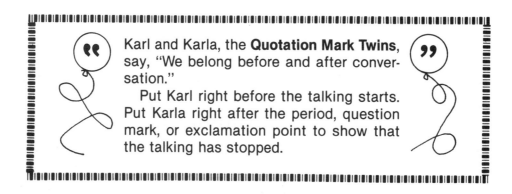

Karl and Karla, the **Quotation Mark Twins**, say, "We belong before and after conversation."

Put Karl right before the talking starts. Put Karla right after the period, question mark, or exclamation point to show that the talking has stopped.

These children are sitting at a table in the school cafeteria. They are eating lunch. Read what each child says.

Name _____

# The Lunch Bunch
## (continued)

Look at the children having lunch on page 24. Copy what each child says on the right line below. Put a comma after the word *says* or a synonym for it. Use the **Quotation Mark Twins** to show what has been said. Put Karl right after the comma and Karla after the period, question mark, or exclamation point. The first one has been done for you.

1.  Kendra exclaims, **"What a great dessert I have today!"** _____

2.  Willis says _____

3.  Marilyn asks _____

4.  Larry declares _____

5.  Sharon asks _____

6.  Bob replies _____

If you were sitting at this lunch table, what would you say to these boys and girls? On the first line below, write your name and a statement you would make. On the second line, write your name and a question you would ask. Don't forget to put the punctuation partners where they are needed.

7.  _____ says _____

8.  _____ asks _____

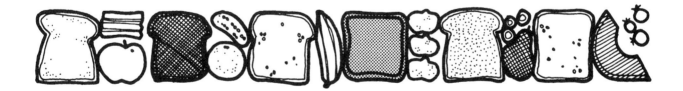

---

### Try This!

Pretend that you and three of your friends are talking about something that is very important to all of you. Write what each person says. Start each sentence with the person's name and the word *says* or a synonym for it. Remember to follow that with **Connie Comma**. Reread the words in the box at the top of page 24, and use the **Quotation Mark Twins** where they are needed.

---

Name _____

# Animal Chatter

It is two hours after closing time at the Animal Crackers Toy Store. The customers, sales clerks, and even the owners have gone home. The stuffed animals are talking among themselves. Imagine what each animal is saying. Then write the conversation on the lines below. Remember to use the **Quotation Mark Twins** before and after each thing that is said. The first one has been done for you.

Barney Bear complains, **"I can't bear this place any longer."** _____

_____ asks Tony Tiger.

Rocky Raccoon replies, _____

Eli Elephant says, _____

Kenny Koala wonders, _____

_____ Monty Monkey exclaims.

Dolly Dolphin adds, _____

Name _____

# Super Sleuth

Detective Devon is out to fool you. On purpose, he has placed a punctuation mistake in each of these sentences. In some sentences, he has left out a punctuation partner that is needed. In other sentences, he has put in the wrong punctuation partner. Be a super sleuth. Find Detective Devon's mistakes. If he has left out a punctuation partner, put it in. If he has used the wrong one, cross it out and write the right one beside it.

1. The suspects were seen leaving the house sometime after midnight

2. Detective Devon asked,  Where were you that night?

3. How many people were involved.

4. What a suspicious-looking character he is.

5. Look at the clear set of fingerprints?

6. What do you think their motive was

7. Detective Devon commented, "This is similar to another case I solved last year?"

8. The witnesses have mysteriously disappeared

9. Were any weapons found at the house.

10. Detective Devon told his assistant, "This case won't be easy to solve "

---

**Try This!**

Play the Super Sleuth game in your class. Divide into two teams. Someone from one team writes a sentence with a punctuation mistake in it on the chalkboard. Members of the other team try to correct the mistake. Allow only three tries. Keep score. Give the team that writes the sentence one point for each wrong guess the other team makes. The winning team is the one with the most points when time is up.

---

Name _____

# Punctuation Stew

Use the recipes on the right to help you cook up a correctly punctuated sentence.
Put the punctuation partners in the right places.

1. Let s go home right now

   1 apostrophe
   1 exclamation point

2. Yes  Andrea drew an eagle that looked lifelike

   1 comma
   1 period

3. We ll see lions  horses  and elephants at

   the circus

   1 apostrophe
   2 commas
   1 period

4. Melissa asked   How far did your frog jump in

   the contest

   1 comma
   quotation marks
   1 question mark
   quotation marks

5. Emily E  Dickinson was born in Amherst  Mass ,

   on Dec  10  1830

   4 periods
   2 commas

6. What a famous poet she was   exclaimed Katie

   quotation marks
   1 exclamation point
   quotation marks
   1 period

7. Brett and Kristin grabbed David s paper airplane

   and flew it out the apt  window

   1 apostrophe
   2 periods

Name _____

# Author's Antics

In this activity, you will have the opportunity to create your own sentences. You may make them silly or serious. Read the sentences below. Notice the blank lines in each one. The symbol on each line tells you what kind of word you need. Look at the three columns of words at the bottom of the page. Choose a word for each blank line by matching the symbols. Write the words you choose on the blank lines in the sentences. After you have completed the sentences, put in the punctuation partners. The number in parentheses after each sentence tells you how many punctuation partners that sentence needs. Opening and closing quotation marks have been counted separately. The first sentence has been done for you.

1. The ● _____purple_____ ▲ _____hippopotamus_____ came

   to school  (1)

2. Weren t you a ▲ _____ for Halloween  (2)

3. My teacher ■ _____ ■ _____

   and ■ _____ every day  (3)

4. On Jan  1  2001, everyone in America will ■ _____  (3)

5. What a ● _____ ▲ _____ that is  (1)

6. Dr  D  Hobsox exclaimed   That ▲ _____

   really ■ _____ rapidly  (6)

| ●Adjectives | ▲Nouns | ■Verbs |
|---|---|---|
| fuzzy | clown | celebrate, celebrates |
| frightened | dancer | dance, dances |
| gigantic | ghost | paint, paints |
| happy | hippopotamus | read, reads |
| noisy | horse | shop, shops |
| purple | mountain | shout, shouts |
| shiny | musician | sing, sings |
| smooth | spider | trot, trots |
| tiny | table | whisper, whispers |
| yellow | witch | whistle, whistles |

Name _____

# My Day

This page is all about you. Write a word or phrase about yourself on each line. Put the right punctuation partner in each circle.

I live in _____ ◯ _____ ◯

On each school morning, I get up at _____ a◯m◯ The first thing I do after

I get up is _____ ◯ Then I _____ ◯

and _____ ◯ For breakfast I eat _____ ◯

_____ ◯ and _____ ◯

When I get to school, I meet my friend _____ ◯

He/She asks ◯◯ _____

_____ ◯◯ We _____

until the bell rings ◯ Then we go to class ◯

My favorite teacher is _____

because _____ ◯

The subjects I like best are _____ ◯

_____ ◯ and _____ ◯

Boy ◯ Do I like _____ ◯ I◯m not

very good at _____ , though ◯ Yes ◯

school is _____ ◯

I◯m dismissed at _____ p◯m◯ I pack my _____ ◯

_____ ◯ and _____ ◯

When I get home, I_____

until it is time for dinner ◯ After dinner I _____ ◯

My bedtime is _____ p◯m◯

# Supplemental Activities

1. Make enough copies of the Punctuation Partner Cards on page 32 for each child to have a set. For added durability, mount the cards on construction paper or tagboard and laminate them or cover them with clear Contact paper. Give each child one card set. Choose a paragraph and read it aloud to the class. Reread it slowly, pausing where punctuation marks are needed. Tell students to hold up the appropriate card or cards each time you pause.

2. Once students are familiar with the Punctuation Partner Cards on page 32 and their use, divide the class into teams of five members. Give one set of Punctuation Partner Cards to each team. Have one member from each team sit or stand in front of the class and hold the set of cards. Choose a paragraph and read it aloud to the class. Reread it slowly, pausing where punctuation marks are needed. The first player to hold up the correct card earns a point for his or her team.

3. Reproduce the Punctuation Partner Cards on page 32 or use the mini-posters on pages 37-48. Make extra copies of the commas and quotation marks. For the latter, indicate by marking or coloring that some are opening quotes (Karl) and some are closing quotes (Karla). Have at least seven students line up facing the rest of the class. Hand each student one card or poster. Read a sentence aloud. Then reread it slowly. When a punctuation mark is needed, have the child with that card or poster hold it overhead or step forward with it. To simplify this activity, hand out only the punctuation marks that will be needed in the sentence you have selected. To make the activity more complex, hand out all of the marks and challenge the children to choose and use only the ones that are needed.

4. Select a paragraph from a student book. Make enough copies so that each child can have one. Hand out the paragraphs and tell children to find and circle all of the periods, commas, question marks, exclamation points, apostrophes, or quotation marks.

5. Print an assortment of simple nouns, verbs, and adjectives on plain index or tagboard cards. Duplicate the Punctuation Partner Cards on page 32. Divide the class into groups. Give each group some word cards and some punctuation cards. Tell the members of each group to work together to construct a sentence and to put the punctuation marks in the proper places.

6. Select a particular punctuation mark and have children write it in color in their sentences, paragraphs, or short stories.

7. Photocopy a paragraph from a student book. Use Liquid Paper to blot out all of the punctuation marks with which students are familiar. Then reproduce the paragraph and hand out one copy to each class member. Tell students to put the Punctuation Partners where they are needed.

# Punctuation Partner Cards

Peter Period

Connie Comma

Quentin Question Mark

Eleanor Exclamation Point

Alfred Apostrophe

Karl    Karla
Quotation Mark Twins

This is to certify that

_____
(student)

has met the
# Punctuation Partners
and mastered
the rules of punctuation.

_____
(teacher)

_____
(date)

# Answer Key

**Page 5, A Word to the Wise**

A word to the wise is enough.
Remember that time is money.
Little strokes fell great oaks.
Lost time is never found again.
There are no gains without pains.
He that riseth late, must trot all day.
A small leak will sink a great ship.
The used key is always bright.
It is hard for an empty sack to stand upright.
Early to bed and early to rise, makes a
man healthy, wealthy, and wise.

**Page 6, Fractured Fortunes (order will vary)**

1. Do not count your chickens before they
   are hatched.
2. Temptation will come your way so be
   on guard.
3. A friend in need is a friend indeed.
4. Success is just around the corner.
5. Good luck does not always repeat itself.
6. You will soon take a voyage.
7. Do not believe people who flatter.
8. You will advance in your chosen field.
9. Be generous and do not hesitate to do
   something nice for someone.

**Page 7, The Portrait Gallery**

Mr. Ted E. Bear
Mrs. Ima T. Vee
Dr. E. Z. Filler
Dr. May Pole
Mr. Sal T. Pretzel
Gov. Bob E. Pin
Mrs. A. Turtle
Prof. Al E. Gator
Sgt. Hersh E. Bar

**Page 8, Ad Venture**

---

### GARAGE SALE
Sat., Oct. 18, 9 a.m.–5 p.m.
100 Sea View Dr.

---

### FREE TO A GOOD HOME
lovable collie, 2 yrs. old, 3712 Chesholm Rd.,
all day Sun.

---

### FOR SALE
5400 sq. ft. warehouse
Fast Buck Realty Co.

---

### FOR RENT
2 bedroom apt., 3 blocks N. of Hunter
Ave. Sch.                    Ph. 964-2852

---

### MR. PINE'S TREE SERVICE
available Mon. - Sat.
reasonable rates
Ph. 968-6530 after 6 p.m.

---

**Page 9, Crack the Code**

1. January 21, 1982
2. November 15, 1880
3. December 16, 1990
4. March 4, 1990
5. April 28, 1972
6. May 1, 1880
7. August 3, 1972
8. July 23, 1990
9. October 21, 1982
10. November 12, 1972

**Pages 10-11, The Picnic Game**

1. Alvin is bringing apple juice.
2. Brad is bringing apple juice and bread.
3. Colleen is bringing apple juice, bread, and
   carrots.
4. Donna is bringing apple juice, bread,
   carrots, and dental floss.
5. Enid is bringing apple juice, bread, carrots,
   dental floss, and eggs.
6. Fritz is bringing apple juice, bread, carrots,
   dental floss, eggs, and frankfurters.

# Answer Key

## (continued)

**Page 12, Travel Time**
1. Boston, Massachusetts
2. New York City, New York
3. Answers will vary.
4. San Francisco, California
5. Paris, France
6. London, England
7. Answers will vary.
8. Answers will vary.
9. Houston, Texas
10. Answers will vary.

**Page 13, Canvassing the Class**
Answers will vary, but each one should start with either *yes* or *no* followed by a comma and then a person's first name.

**Page 14, Meet Connie Comma**
Hi! My name is Constance Comma. My friends call me Connie, Con, or C.C. I was born in Juneau, Alaska. I moved to Anchorage when I was three. My birthday is February 29, 1980. I celebrate it on March 1 when it's not Leap Year. I'll be twenty years old on February 29, 2000. Peter Period, Alfred Apostrophe, Quentin Question Mark, Eleanor Exclamation Point, and the Quotation Mark Twins are my best friends. We love to party, play, and punctuate. Yes, I enjoy being a punctuation partner.

**Page 15, Scrambled Sentences**
1. Birds raised for meat and eggs are called poultry.
2. Some poultry animals are chickens, turkeys, geese, and ducks.
3. Chicken eggs take twenty days to hatch.
4. Yes, each person in the U.S. eats an average of 41 lbs. of poultry each year.

**Page 16, Riddle Me**
*How does an elephant get down from a tree?* It sits on a leaf and waits until fall.
*What does a worm do in a corn field?* It goes in one ear and out another.
*What did one owl say to the other owl?* I don't give a hoot about you.
*What has a heel, a toe, a leg, and nothing else?* A stocking does.
*What did Delaware?* She wore a New Jersey.
*What did the scissors say to the barber?* It won't be long now.
*Why did Silly Sally put her father in the refrigerator?* She wanted a cold pop.

**Page 16, Riddle Me (continued)**
*Who can raise things without lifting them?* A farmer can.
*What is black and white and red all over?* A sunburned zebra is
*What is the best way to keep fish from smelling?* Cut off their noses.

**Page 17, Bus Banter**
What is the bus driver's name?
Are we almost there?
We're missing recess.
Where are we going?
Can we open a window?
I'm getting hungry.
Why are we stopping?
I forgot my lunch.

**Page 18, Stormy Weather**
1. How dark the room is!
2. Look at that lightning!
3. The thunder is rattling the windows!
4. Boy, am I scared!
5. Listen to the wind howl!
6. This is really exciting!
7-10. Answers will vary but should be sentences that show strong feeling and are followed by exclamation points.

**Page 19, Cartoon Capers**
1. Hit the road!
2. Look at that square dance!
3. Now that's a *real* bookworm!
4. Don't make a spectacle of yourself!

**Page 20, A Twist of the Tongue**
1. Did Darby dive down deep during December?
2. Every eligible elephant eats eggs Easter evening.
3. Will Willie and Wilma wind their way west?
4. Tina the Terrible took twenty tadpoles today.
5. What a wily walrus Waldo was!
6. Should Steve sell seventeen small-sized shirts?
7. Mischievous Miles makes mud mountains most Mondays.
8. Barnaby Badger bowed bashfully before busloads of bankers.
9. How happily Harriet Hippo and Herbert Hedgehog harmonized!
10. Can cunning Carlos calm cantankerous Carmen?

# Answer Key
## (continued)

### Pages 21–22, At the Pet Show
1. Heidi's
2. Mark's
3. Kevin's
4. Leah's
5. David's
6. Julia's
7. Elana's
8. Corie's
9. Bernie's
10. Kyle's

### Page 23, Will You Be Mine?
1. Won't you be my Valentine?
2. I'm yours. Be mine.
3. Let's get together.
4. We're quite a pair!
5. You're the greatest!
6. I'll always be stuck on you.

### Pages 24–25, The Lunch Bunch
1. Kendra exclaims, "What a great dessert I have today!"
2. Willis says, "My taco needs more cheese."
3. Marilyn asks, "Do you like tuna sandwiches?"
4. Larry declares, "What a messy eater Bob is!"
5. Sharon asks, "Do you want my chocolate cake?"
6. Bob replies, "I'll trade you my pear for it."

### Page 26, Animal Chatter
Answers will vary but should include quotation marks and correct end punctuation (period, question mark, or exclamation point).

### Page 27, Super Sleuth
1. The suspects were seen leaving the house sometime after midnight.
2. Detective Devon asked, "Where were you that night?"
3. How many people were involved?
4. What a suspicious-looking character he is!
5. Look at the clear set of fingerprints!
6. What do you think their motive was?
7. Detective Devon commented, "This is similar to another case I solved last year."
8. The witnesses have mysteriously disappeared.
9. Were any weapons found at the house?
10. Detective Devon told his assistant, "This case won't be easy to solve."

### Page 28, Punctuation Stew
1. Let's go home right now!
2. Yes, Andrea drew an eagle that looked lifelike.
3. We'll see lions, horses, and elephants at the circus.
4. Melissa asked, "How far did your frog jump in the contest?"
5. Emily E. Dickinson was born in Amherst, Mass., on Dec. 10, 1830.
6. "What a famous poet she was!" exclaimed Katie.
7. Brett and Kristin grabbed David's paper airplane and flew it out the apt. window.

### Page 29, Author's Antics
1. The purple hippopotamus came to school.
2. Weren't you a ▲ for Halloween?
3. My teacher ■ , ■ , and ■ every day.
4. On Jan. 1, 2001, everyone in America will ■ .
5. What a ● ▲ that is!
6. Dr. D. Hobsox exclaimed, "That ▲ really ■ rapidly!"

### Page 30, My Day
I live in _____⊙_____⊙
On each school morning, I get up at _____ a⊙m⊙
The first thing I do after I get up is _____⊙
Then I _____ and _____⊙ For
breakfast I eat _____⊙_____⊙
and _____⊙
When I get to school, I meet my friend _____⊙
He/She asks⊙"_____?" We _____
until the bell rings ⊙ Then we go to class ⊙
My favorite teacher is _____
because ____⊙ The subjects I like best are ____⊙
_____⊙ and _____⊙ Boy ! Do I
like _____ ! I'm not very good
at _____ , though ⊙ Yes ⊙ school
is _____ ⊙
I'm dismissed at _____ p⊙m⊙ I pack my
_____⊙_____⊙ and _____⊙
When I get home, I _____ until it is time
for dinner ⊙ After dinner I _____ ⊙ My
bedtime is _____ p⊙m⊙

# Peter Period

# Peter Period

# Connie Comma

Connie Comma

Put me after each item in a series except the last one.

Punctuation Partners
© 1983 - The Learning Works, Inc.

# Connie Comma

Put me between the name of a city or town and the name of a state or country.

# Eleanor
# Exclamation Point

# The Quotation Mark Twins

We belong before and after conversation.
Put Karl right before the talking starts.
Put Karla right after the period,
question mark, or exclamation point
to show that the talking has stopped.

Karl

Karla